The Author

Andrew Wilson lives in Devon (UK) with his wife Barbara and son Lucas. Andrew has spent the last 20 years improving productivity for blue chip organisations worldwide. In 2000 he founded the company Finidhyn Ltd. in order to help organisations improve their operational performance.

Andrew is an associate lecturer for the Open University, a published author, an orator and expert in management systems and complexity science; he leads the way in creative and dynamic thinking in global management circles.

Andrew can be contacted at aw@finidhyn.com or skyped at awfinidhyn.

Website: www.finidhyn.com

Linkedin: http://uk.linkedin.com/in/finidhyn

Productivity

What it is, and how to measure it

Andrew Wilson

Lulu Publishing

Lulu Publishing

First published in the United Kingdom 2011

ISBN: 978-1-4478-0923-4

This book is dedicated to my beautiful wife, Barbara, without whom I would have fallen at the first hurdle, and my son, Lucas, who brings light into my day.

CONTENTS

Acknowledgements

My thanks to Barbara, my editor at Southmoor Editing. I freely admit to being more than a little cavalier with the English language, and my punctuation veers from the creative to the non-existent. Without her careful ministrations, you would be reading a less coherent version of this book.

"Strategy fails, not through a lack of imagination, but rather a lack of good implementation."

Andrew Wilson, 2011

INTRODUCTION

> *"Productivity, along with being an extremely important metric in all of our daily lives, is a journey the foundation of which is always 'output'."*

Henry Ford

If you are reading this book, then one of two things will have happened, I suspect: either you will have been given the book by your organisation in an attempt to introduce you to the topic of productivity, or you may have come across it lying around in someone's book shelf. You will undoubtedly wonder why anyone would ever write a book on a subject which, on first glance, is so basic and obvious.

For ten years we have run our business website www.finidhyn.com and reviewed the weekly activity reports relating to the site. In those ten years we have counted almost 15,000 views and downloads of a short explanatory article on "Productivity and how to measure it". Despite all of the other content relating to advanced management tools, this seemed to be a recurring feature of visits to our site. We have had downloads throughout the world on this subject, and it occurred to me that despite the basic nature of the subject, it is one that we all need.

As emerging economies become larger and more industrial, the need for productivity improvement and measurement will grow too. Also, in developed countries, where a new generation of managers are taking over the reigns of established businesses, there is a constant need for renewal of basic skills.

I looked high and low for a book like this and couldn't find one; it then made sense why our article on productivity was so popular.

You might see this book as a basic introduction to a simple enough subject, but do not underestimate its importance in the modern world. All of the advanced tools and techniques hawked around the market place today are all, at some level, dependent on the basics such as productivity being in place already.

What is productivity? We know inherently that to be more productive we need to do more with less. In essence, we are on a continuous journey within our working lives to be more productive.

The purpose of this book is simple: to give you, the reader, an insight into the world of productivity measurement in order that you can become a champion of this measure within your organisation.

Chapter 1

FADS AND FASHIONS

"A good deal of corporate planning ... is like a ritual rain dance. It has no effect on the weather that follows, but those who engage in it think it does. ... Moreover, much of the advice related to corporate planning is directed at improving the dancing, not the weather."

Brian Quinn, Dartmouth University

"Lean Manufacturing", "Six Sigma", "Agile Manufacturing", and many of the other tools hawked around the market place are all legitimate improvement methodologies. Rarely, if ever, has a senior manager been dismissed for embarking upon a new initiative using one of these tools.

Modern business is defined by the almost constant application of management tools in an attempt to improve profitability though increased quality, reduced cost and improved operational performance. What is frustrating about the plethora of tool kits is that many initiatives fail due to the lack of basic business foundations within the companies where the initiative is tried. As a result of trying to implement these tools in environments that are not ready for them, the tools fail and the organisation goes in search of another one that might deliver better results. It is for this reason that we have come to regard many of these tools as "fads and fashions".

Philosophically, all of these tools and techniques are directed at one thing: productivity and the increase thereof. Yet it is precisely this productivity measure which is missing in so many businesses today. If productivity were present as a measure in business, then there would be a high likelihood that the basic data infrastructure required to support these more advanced tools would be present.

It is as a result of our aversion to productivity measurement that we find ourselves bemoaning the lack of "sustainability" with regard to results in business today.

It is worth mentioning at this stage that I do not support the current discussion on sustainability in industry. A discussion on sustainability inherently pre-supposes failure or a propensity to fail. In fact, why would anyone wish to sustain a level of performance. Surely, the correct ambition would be to continue to improve performance beyond the current level and to continue to do so. So, for the purposes of this book, I would like to make it clear that I support a policy of "continuous improvement" with which I pre-suppose success.

I would not want you to leave this chapter thinking that I am not advocating the use of many of the "tools and techniques" we have mentioned. What I am saying is that they are all limited in their usefulness unless they have been built upon a secure foundation. Many of the success stories written as a result of using these tools are describing situations in organisations where sound basic business metrics are a way of life and the foundations of good data are securely in place. It is easy to forget that much of the success of a new technique owes a great deal to an incredible amount of hard work accomplished before it is implemented.

So, if I wish to make any statement at all on these management techniques it is this: all management techniques are valid within certain organisational contexts and will deliver differing levels of results, dependent on the level of operational performance already attained within an organisation. What none of these techniques can do is drive long term productive growth without sound operational fundamentals, one of which is productivity.

One should not forget that the majority, if not all, of these management tools are directed at one thing and one thing only: increasing productivity. In the following chapters, I aim to show you how prevalent and all encompassing this concept of productivity is, and the benefits that can be accrued through its adoption and use.

Chapter 2

STANDARDS

"Every number 9 shoe in the country ought to be of the same length. A quart ought to be a quart, and a pound ought to be a pound. To that extent standardisation is a convenience and a help to progress."

Henry Ford, *"Today and Tomorrow"*, 1926

We are not about to launch into ethics or morality here; although they are important, they are not for this book. The standards I am talking about are work standards. Once upon a time, the study of standards in the workplace was called "Time-and-Motion" but in our modern, caring and socially aware world we don't use stop-watches anymore in case we upset people. As a result, employee happiness is at an all time low due to overwork and stress. Why? Well, precisely because we are such sensitive souls. If we were to put away our sensitive natures and, instead, get each other to measure our work accurately, we might find that in many cases we are trying to fit 10 days work into 5 - and we can't do that on a sustainable basis.

So, when I talk about standards, I am talking about the foundation block of work. I am aware that this recourse to measurement may not be to everyone's liking in today's business world, but I would ask you to bear with me on this journey. In 20 years, I have never made anyone's job harder or more stressful by implementing standards of work in an organisation. If anything, introducing standards makes companies quieter, less stressful, more profitable and ultimately happier places in which to work.

Consider for a moment all the aspects of your everyday life where you come across standards: trains, planes, distances, weights, time, volumes, and many, many more. What would our world be like if we did not have standard measures? It would make buying a kilo of rice almost impossible, as we would all have to negotiate what we thought our definition of a kilo was for a start. The same applies to things such as time. Most of us give our skills to our jobs for a set amount of time and in return are paid a wage for doing so. We define this relationship in terms of time (measured in years, months, weeks, days, hours, minutes and seconds), skill (measured in doctorates, degrees, HNDs, A' Levels, O' Levels), and pay (thousands, hundreds, tens of pounds): all aspects of our working lives are defined by standards. So, why then do we pull back from analysing and measuring our work in amongst all of these standards?

Every day, millions of us go to work and sit down at a desk where no standards other than "pleasing your boss" have been established. One day your boss wants overtime and 200% effort, the next day he or she couldn't care less. "Oh!" you will doubtlessly cry, "but what about flexibility?" Well, flexibility just means you have spare time, or will give your own time freely. In fact, it validates the entire position I have taken so far in this book; the complete lack of standards. You cannot have flexibility if, for example, you have the correct amount of work for 8 hours of work each day; being flexible in this scenario just means you will get behind on the work you have stopped doing in order to do something else for someone else. When you look at it like this it is very hard to see why employees wouldn't demand a time and motion study of their work within the organisation. What we tend to find is that the overworked welcome the study and the underworked resist the study. This kind of reaction is not one we should celebrate: knowing that your friendly work colleagues couldn't care less about your welfare, as long as they don't have to do any more work!

What are Standards?

Standards should be the only static part of a business. You may have heard the old adage that "the only constant in modern business is change". Well, that is, or should be, with the exception of standards. There is a very good reason for this from a business perspective, and anyone who has tried to reconcile a P&L account off the back of any of the commercial accounting packages on the market, and failed, will attest to this view. The problems which many of these systems struggle with are fluctuating variable costs and the management of the difference between the time and price goods are bought at and the time they are used.

The cost of inputs such as raw materials and utilities fluctuate from day to day, week to week and month to month. This causes variances to exist between the budgeted costs and the actual costs, and between the forecasted costs and the actual costs. Unfortunately, included within all of this is labour and performance with regard to the manufacturing side of the operation. Finance departments are adept at estimating the usage of raw materials in a monthly cycle but, unfortunately, operations tend to be less skilled in doing so. There is a tendency to believe that the accounts are the gospel truth, but this would be a mistake, as there are some basic assumptions at work in most accounting packages (e.g. that materials are costed by batch in the month in which they are bought, due to the need to reconcile the purchasing loop). The problem occurs when production use materials which fall outside the purchasing calculation loop. This can happen for a variety of reasons, such as missing stock on a stock check or receiving more (or less) than was ordered. These scenarios should seem all too familiar to the production manager who has to defend material variances at the end of each month. Not only does the production manager work with different numbers in the form of operational indicators but also, if he is not working to standards, he cannot tell the finance guys which part of the variance belongs to performance loss against standard (i.e. a production issue) and which part of the problem relates to finance.

If this seems a little far fetched, you will be surprised to hear that in almost every situation where I have had to put in operational standards and reporting systems, I have, within months, been able to identify the margin of error with which the finance department is working. You see, at the end of the year the finance department gets an opportunity to do the "big reconciliation" in the end-of-year figures, but from month to month their estimates sometimes move around considerably depending on events within the business. Being able to correct those numbers for finance not only helps finance, it also helps you.

Standards, therefore, are a reference point upon which you can start to build your operational reporting. The single most important aspect of operational standards is that they are based on numbers that do not fluctuate. For example, if my standard usage of screws in a product is 4 screws per item, then my usage is a function of volume only, and not price. However, if I were to measure the screws as £4 per item produced, I would have to make allowances for cost fluctuations and then estimate waste and allocate the correct cost to that. I have seen this done with unerring frequency, and it makes life very difficult indeed.

The philosophy businesses should adopt is one of allocating the correct measures to the correct departments. For example, in production, operational ratios are all that should bother a production manager - after all a production manager is responsible only for the conversion ratios of raw materials into saleable product. Procurement are responsible for the acquisition of those raw materials at least cost, and finance are responsible for reporting the cost of operational variances in production as a result of price fluctuations and expenditure versus income received. I have seen more time wasted by businesses through the incorrect allocation of operational and financial ratios within the business structure than almost anything else.

For example, take a production manager's KPIs: productivity, quality, waste. If he/she continues to convert raw materials to finished product whilst hitting his or her target ratios, there is little or no need for their further involvement in any financial discussion relating to shop floor performance other than expenditure relating to overtime use. Building on this argument, there is a much bigger role for standards and that is their role in the definition of the business model you are running.

When a business is created, it is set-up according to a set of assumptions. These assumptions are, effectively, standards relating to the cost of providing a service or product in relation to the price that is going to be charged for the items. If a business successfully achieves these standards then the business will be profitable, if it doesn't it will be less profitable.

Chapter 3

STANDARDS IN PRODUCTION ENVIRONMENTS

There are three approaches to establishing standards within a production environment. These approaches relate to the different types of production environment you may have. In general, there are three types:

1) Fixed Speed, Fixed Labour;
2) Flexible Speed, Flexible Labour;
3) Flexible Speed, Fixed Labour.

It may not be immediately obvious what I mean by this, so I shall elaborate with some examples.

Fixed Speed, Fixed Labour

An example of "Fixed Speed, Fixed Labour" would be an automotive manufacturing plant and derivatives thereof. The reason for this is that at the start of each year an automotive plant will decide how many cars it needs to make for the coming year, and will divide the available time for production by the required output to establish a "Takt time" or "drum beat". This is the rate at which finished product needs to come off the end of the line in order to meet the target at the end of the year. By defining the output required for the year and the rate of production in order to achieve this output, the automotive manufacturer in effect fixes both the speed and the labour requirements for the plant at the outset.

Therefore, for this type of manufacturer the only thing of real interest from a performance point-of-view is downtime and its avoidance, as it is the only thing that will constrain output. There is very little flexibility relating to labour, as there is a set amount required in order to run the production line. So, barring some overtime and holiday cover, the labour bill should be very stable. In these types of production environments, if your production line goes down for an hour and you don't make five cars as a result, you have lost those five cars forever, because it is impossible to speed the line up, and too complex and costly to re-lay the line for a faster "Takt time".

A visual representation of the discussion above can be seen below.

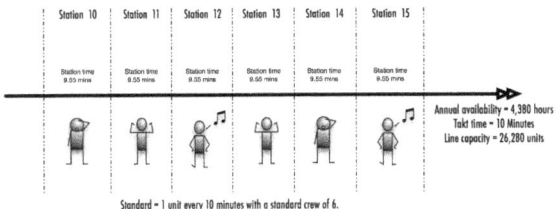

Standard = 1 unit every 10 minutes with a standard crew of 6.

Flexible Speed, Flexible Labour

Examples of "Flexible Speed, Flexible Labour" tend to be found in the FMCG (Fast Moving Consumer Goods) industry. Here, multiple variants of product, which may differ in labelling and/or packaging but share a similar core process, are sent down similar production lines. These products may differ in run speed and crewing, depending on what product variant is being run at the time.

The food industry is a good example of this model, along with home-care liquid bottling and micro-electronics. In some industries, especially those which target low cost markets, the labour content of a product relative to all input costs is high; therefore, a drop in productivity can have a substantial negative impact on gross margin. A good example of this might be a depositing line; this may be bottling or pies, it applied in both cases. If you set the line up for small pies or bottles, the line will run at a certain speed for a defined crew. If you then switch over to large pies or bottles, the rate of production may drop and the required crew to man the line may also decrease. The key aspect to "Flexible Speed, Flexible Labour" is that this production model tends to predominate in rapidly changing commercial environments and, as such, the mix effect within the business has a substantial effect on performance and capacity.

Whereas the car plant model, mentioned above in our "Fixed Speed, Fixed Labour" example, created a production line with a predetermined labour requirement, the "Flexible Speed, Flexible Labour" models of the FMCG sector are flexing their labour up to +/- 40% on a daily or weekly basis depending on demand and mix. This flexing and labour management becomes extremely difficult in industries requiring skilled labour. There is a correlation between the cost of the product produced and the flexibility of the labour. As a general rule, where the cost of the product in finished goods terms is high, and labour is a smaller percentage of the overall cost of the product, then there is a tendency not to flex the labour, but, instead, to invest in the upskilling of that labour. However, this makes these businesses vulnerable to demand fluctuations. As a result, knowing your standards and measuring performance closely are critical to all areas in these business types.

A visual representation of the discussion above can be seen below.

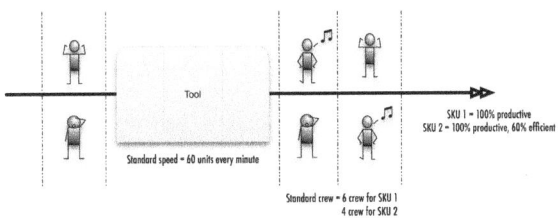

Flexible Speed, Fixed Labour

The final category of production relates to "Fixed Labour, Flexible Speed". This type of manufacturing tends to be specialist manufacturing with defined skill sets, producing bespoke or customised products. One of the best examples I have seen of this type of manufacturing is patisserie production. Here, one line with a defined crew will make five or six different types of patisserie, and each product will be made at a different speed, depending on the complexity and the nature of the product. The speed is defined by the process and not the line or machinery, although sometimes a machine may well undertake one step in a multiple step process. In these types of environments setting standards is a much harder job, as each line and station's work needs to be broken down and timed. Line balancing is necessary in order to ensure that all staff are equally loaded with work. Finally, the end of line production rate can be calculated, thus allowing you to arrive at a standard for one product.

There are similarities between this category and "Flexible Speed, Flexible Labour", in as far as if you change the labour on the production line in this category you will change the output rate at the end of the line. There is, however, a major difference in this category and that is the reliance on skill, which results in an inflexibility of labour. Due to the dependence on the skill of the staff in this model, the setting of standards is actually more about capacity planning and scheduling. In this category, you have to optimise the crew as a function of all the processes in the business. So, you would look at total work to be done throughout the factory and the capacity required by the factory to meet the average sales and, as a result, set the standard crews so that labour is optimised across all processes and the fixed level of labour is capable of delivering the capacity required. This is quite a different proposition as a manufacturing model compared to the other models discussed previously.

A visual representation of the discussion above can be seen below.

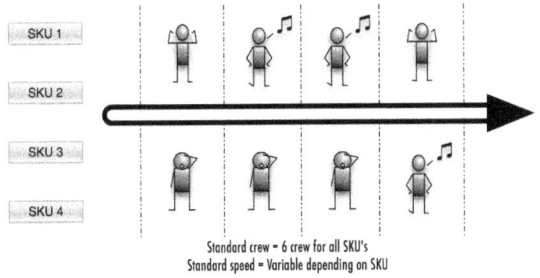

Standard crew = 6 crew for all SKU's
Standard speed = Variable depending on SKU

Chapter 4

STANDARDS IN NON-PRODUCTION ENVIRONMENTS

"The difficulty is how to replace Homo Faber with a new kind of man. He will not be man the maker any longer. He will be man the steersman – of large complex, interactive systems."

Stafford Beer, 1975

Setting standards in service environments, which are dominated by administrative tasks, does appear, at first glance, to be a very different proposition to that of a manufacturing shop floor, where there are discrete machines, which perform designated tasks at pre-determined speeds. However, administrative environments and production environments are more similar than they first appear. Both environments require machines and people to process work in order to produce something. In a manufacturing environment you usually end up with a product you can touch and see; in an administrative environment you often end up with a product or service, but the manifestation of this is sometimes more abstract. It may be that the end-result of a service is a barcode or a reference number if booking a flight on an aeroplane, or a certificate reference number if it is an insurance document. The important thing to understand is that in both environments a series of predetermined steps of work need to take place, at a predetermined rate, in order to produce an output. As a result, it is possible to measure productivity. The first step, as with production environments, is to establish the standards for the work.

Within administrative or service environments, standard setting, as I mentioned, is not as clear-cut as in production environments. This is because work tends to be heterogeneous by nature and, therefore, does not lend itself easily to classification or measurement. However, you will be surprised by the extent to which measurement is possible and how it can help in the balancing of work within these environments.

A standard can be almost any unit of measurement: time, quantity, distance, weight, etc. For example, if your job is to enter purchasing invoices into a database, you will have a number of mandatory fields to fill in on the computer and an element of filing with regard to the paper copies. If you have all the information to hand, and no one interrupts you whilst you input the data, it might take an average of 4 minutes to enter all the data into the computer system. At the end of the day when you come to file all of your paper copies, you might file 100 invoices in an hour, at an average rate of 1 invoice per 1 minute 40 seconds. So, assuming no interruptions, an invoice takes an average of 5 minutes and 40 seconds to process from beginning to end. You now have a standard for the processing of a purchasing invoice.

Now let us assume that you work an 8-hour day. How much of the 8 hours is available as productive time? There will be time during the day that you are not at your desk working: breaks for lunch and the odd cup of tea and perhaps the odd meeting. All of these things will take you away from processing invoices. Therefore, it is necessary to take some time away from the 8 hours that you are in work for these diversions. In this example we might decide to take one hour off the 8 hours in order to cover these indirect activities. As a result of this allowance you are left with a working day for processing procurement invoices of 7 hours, or 420 minutes.

In order to arrive at a standard output for a day's work, it is necessary to divide the available time (420 minutes) by the total time to process an invoice, which in this case is 5 minutes and 40 seconds. This would indicate that your standard day's work is (420/5.66)=74 invoices a day.

Remember that you are not trying to estimate a total productivity figure for this role at the moment; you are just trying establish a standard for the processing of invoices.

Now that you have a series of standards, it is really easy to see if you have too much or too little work to do. It's not open to negotiation or interpretation anymore; it's quite simply a fact. If you processed 50 invoices in the 7 hours today, you were only 67% productive; if you processed 100 invoices in 7 hours, you were 135% productive, which means you measured yourself incorrectly when you were setting the standard. In this example, where we have only used 1 person as the standard for the work done, the productivity and efficiency figure will be the same.

Ideally, your standard should be the fastest possible time you can accomplish a task. The rationale for this is that it is impossible for people to work at the fastest speed all day, but it is good to know what the "burst speed" (i.e. unsustainable speed) of a process is, as it allows you some flexibility from time to time if there is a little more work to be accomplished than is normal.

A normal work rate should be in the region of 80% of maximum, and should be a comfortable rate of work that you can maintain all day long without getting overly fatigued and making mistakes. It is possible to work faster, but it is not necessarily desirable, as mistakes will be made which you will have to go back and fix, and that will prevent you from working productively.

So, taking this example to a logical conclusion, if you are employed in the role of data entry clerk and the standard work rate is 80% of 74 invoices per working day, your expected daily invoice completion rate is $74*0.8 = 60$ invoices.

If an employee has 240 days a year available (with 20 days holiday taken out), then you can expect to process 14,400 invoices a year. If you currently process 29,000 invoices, you need to employ 2 people.

See how easy it is! Now, isn't this a better of approaching things?

Chapter 5

CALCULATING PRODUCTIVITY IN PRODUCTION ENVIRONMENTS

> *"Different operations take, ... unequal periods, and yield therefore, in equal times unequal quantities of fractional products. If, therefore, the same labourer has, day after day, to perform the same operation, there must be a different number of labourers for each operation; for instance, in type manufacture, there are four founders and two breakers to one rubber: the founder casts 2,000 type an hour, the breaker breaks up 4,000, and the rubber polishes 8,000."*

Karl Marx, 1867

Productivity, or some measure of output relating to resource usage, is prevalent in almost every manufacturing environment you enter - and so it should be. After all, manufacturers are in the business of making things, so knowing how much you made is important. However, gone are the days when a manufacturing manager oversaw a dozen or more staff on a single production line producing one or two products. In today's manufacturing world, companies can employ thousands of staff, producing thousands of different products, on thousands of pieces of equipment. As a result of this scale and complexity, a proper measure of productivity is required, which allows accurate measurement irrespective of changes in volume, product mix, or packaging and labour changes.

There is a story I was once told, which I am sure is apocryphal, and yet resonates in today's world of manufacturing, and it goes along the lines of this:

"In the old Soviet Union, there existed a factory which was responsible for making nails for the whole country. Each year a member of the Politburo responsible for industrial output would look at the nation's nail requirement and place an order with the factory for however many tonnes of nails this translated into. This annual order would be the target the factory would be required to produce for the year. Each year, however, the factory failed to meet

its output target, and so each year the director of the factory was replaced with a new incumbent. This continued until one year the factory hit its required tonnage exactly. The man in the Politburo hired a plane and went out from Moscow to see how this remarkable feat had been achieved. On arrival, he was shown to the plant director's office and congratulations were passed around. The man from the Politburo was then led to the rear of the factory to see this output - and was presented with 1 two hundred and fifty tonne nail!"

The moral of this story is: be careful which measurements you use.

Fundamentally, productivity is a combination of two measures: that of efficiency and that of labour utilisation. From time to time you may hear it being called labour efficiency. It is, as far as I know, the only accurate and robust measure which describes the relationship between efficiency (output) and the quantity of labour used in the production of that output.

The formula for productivity is shown below and is described as the total Earned Standard Labour Hours (ESLH) for a given period of time of production, divided by the total hours paid for in order to have achieved that period of production or output.

$$\sum \left[\frac{ESLH}{Actual\ Hours} \right]$$

As I mentioned in the last chapter, you will need a standard or series of standards upon which to base your measurement. As you will see later, when we talk about calculating Return on Capital Employed (ROCE), there is a correct way of establishing these standards.

When you buy a production line, you will buy a line capable of producing whatever widget you are trying to make at the time, and you will buy a line capable of making a certain number of these widgets at a certain speed. For example, if you were buying a line to make apple pies, you would consider how many pies you needed in total for the year, and how much of the market for apple pies you were likely to gain in the coming years. This data would form the basis of the information you would use to buy the production line. Potentially, you would buy a line capable of making this year's demand easily with two or three times the capacity for future years' growth. You would cost this equipment and run a discounted cash flow to estimate the pay back time or ROCE for the purchase. Any purchase of large scale manufacturing equipment requires a lot of time, effort and money in order to ensure you buy the right machine for the job.

Let us say, for example, that the machine we decide to buy can make 20 apple pies a minute. These apple pies are of a certain size and weight. We bought this machine because we required an annual production volume which equated to one 8-hour shift of production by the machine, for 5 days a week, at 20 apple pies a minute. The new line requires 11 staff to run it, at 20 apple pies a minute. These staff members have various jobs relating to functions on the line, from the person responsible for unpacking the apple sauce and filling the hopper at the front of the line, to the pallet puller, responsible for removing finished product at the end of line. The crew of 11 people is the "standard crew" required to run the line making the standard apple pie.

This information now forms the basis of the standard for this line in relation to the one product we are currently running down it. We know that the standard speed of the line is 20 pies a minute and we need 11 people to run it.

This is where we can now start to construct the productivity measure.

At its most basic, productivity answers the question:

How many man-minutes of labour should I use to produce a certain volume of product at a standard speed, how many did I actually use and what is the ratio thereof?

In order to do this, we need to create a measure of how many man-minutes we should use. This is known in the trade as "Earned Standard Labour Hours", or ESLH for short. ESLH is the number of minutes the staff on the line accrue at standard speed and crewing for the quantity of product they make. So, if you were to make 10,000 apple pies you would calculate your ESLH with the following calculation:

$$\sum \left[\frac{\textit{Units produced}}{\textit{Standard units per unit of production time}} \right]$$

The time it should have taken you to do the job (the standard time) is 10,000 units divided by the standard machine rate of 20 units per minute, which gives you 500 minutes. Basically, what you are doing here is simply dividing the 10,000 units by how many you make a minute, to give you the number of minutes you need to run the machine to make 10,000 units.

In order to arrive at how many standard labour minutes you should have used (the minutes that you <u>should</u> have to pay for) you multiply the standard time by the standard crew of 11; this gives you 5,500 minutes, or 91.6 hours. I have underlined the 'should' above, because this calculation shows you how many minutes you would pay for, in theory, if you were to run at standard speed with a standard crew; it does not represent the number of minutes you might actually pay for in practice.

You have now calculated that if the machine were to run continuously for 500 minutes (or 8.3 hours) at the standard speed, you should end up with 10,000 apple pies, and you should only have to pay for Earned Standard Labour Hours of 91.6 hours of labour.

With the calculation above you have managed to convert the standard time and standard labour, that we discussed originally, into an aggregate measure, which tells you how much you should spend in time and money on labour to deliver a predetermined quantity of apple pies.[1]

The next step is to construct the full Key Performance Indicator (KPI) for productivity by simply dividing the standard hours (you should have paid for) by the actual hours (you ended up paying for). This is shown in the following calculation:

$$Productivity = \sum \left[\frac{ESLH}{Actual\ Hours} \right]$$

What really happened?

Reality rarely runs to standards, but it is precisely because we have a standard measurement that we are able to compare theory with practice, and this is, at its most basic, what the productivity measurement is. In the following example we shall run through the calculation with numbers relating to what actually happened.

Your standard staffing for the line was 11 people but you used 12 staff and you ran for 620 minutes rather than the 500 minutes as planned.

So, actual labour time is 620*12 = 7,440 labour minutes , or 124 labour hours.

Therefore, our productivity is (5500/7440)*100 = 74%

This means that you used 26% more labour than you required.

You know this either by subtracting 74% from 100% or from the following calculation: 7440-5500 = 1940, and consequently 1940/7440 = 26%. Either way, at an average hourly rate of £10 per hour for the staff on the line, it cost you £323.3 more than it should have done, and that has just come straight off the bottom line.[2] If you continue like that for the rest of the year, 7 days a week, it will cost you £117,693.30.

What you now need to look at in detail is how, or why, 26% more labour was used. You know that you had an extra person on the line and that should pose the question, "Why?", but there is no way that person cost £323 for the day (8.3 hours at £10 is £83), so something else has happened to influence the productivity measure. You can see that the line ran for 120 minutes more than it should have done, thus increasing the time which everyone had to work and get paid. That, plus the extra person, is what accounts for the increase of £323.

You can now see how much useful information is available to you by setting a simple standard, from which you can compare your performance. In chapter 7, on downtime, we'll be looking at some of the other information which will be useful to know when trying to understand why our apple pie line ran at only 74% productivity.

Chapter 6

CALCULATING PRODUCTIVITY IN NON-PRODUCTION ENVIRONMENTS

I think that it is the rise of the service-based economy, which has led to the general demise of productivity as a measure. Based on many years of trying to implement productivity measures in service-based industries, I have found that people have negative associations with time-and-motion studies. I think this is due to an association which many people make between time-and-motion type studies and job losses. I do sympathise with this view for three reasons. Firstly, it is entirely because time-and-motion has been ignored that businesses end up with the incorrect staffing and, as a result, when they finally do take a scientific approach to the work, they are forced to cut back in many areas. This is a paradox of the modern age. Secondly, because time-and-motion has traditionally been associated with manufacturing environments, people tend to feel that they have escaped it when they manage to graduate off the shop floor and move into an administrative position. In addition, some people brought up in the professions would never conceive of applying an apparent "working-man's measure" to their sophisticated and multi-faceted working lives. Thirdly, and probably most importantly, many people will argue that it is a lot harder to measure productivity in an administrative and managerial environment. I have some sympathy for this point-of-view but, rather than throw the baby out with the bath water, I have seen the very positive effects of this methodology when it is applied systematically and intelligently within service environments. Indeed, in defence of time-and-motion, I would say that if we had persevered with the measure in modern service businesses, we would undoubtedly have substantially improved the services being offered today.

In today's business world, where we are subjected to continuous performance appraisals and grading with 360 degree feedback, one of the things that puzzles me most is the substantial difference between the job description most of us have and the reality of our working lives. In practice, I find that when you sit an employee down and ask them to describe their job and what their responsibilities are, you will rarely find much of a correlation between what you are told and their job description - if they have one. In fact, I often find that one of the biggest contributors to work place stress is the confusion for employees due to the difference between what is expected of them and what their actual role in the business is. Very often, simple clarification and boundary setting will lead to much greater output and a happier employee, but to do this a level of measurement must take place.

In a similar way to a manufacturing process, there will be a core process and ancillary processes within the delivery of a service offering.[3] Each offering is akin to an SKU (Stock Keeping Unit) in a production environment. In most administrative environments you have a "Fixed Labour, Flexible Speed" arrangement, with discrete offerings taking different lengths of time and resource in the process of their delivery. It is for this reason that the capacity planning of the business is reliant on a more or less predetermined mix of offerings through the organisation. If the mix were to change then the capacity of the organisation to deliver the new mix of offerings would change accordingly. Normally the first sign of a change of mix and a negative impact on capacity is when work starts to back-up, or when the waiting times on phonecalls coming into the business start to increase. Unfortunately, many businesses do not have productivity as a measure and, therefore, assume that the backing-up of orders is simply a supply and demand issue. As a result, they just tend to throw labour at the problem. In many cases this is not the correct reaction; often the change in volume and mix is transitory due to promotional activity, or the capacity constraint is caused by re-work due to process failings.

The important point being made here is that if you have not broken down your business process(s) into standard units of work, and you are not measuring productivity, you will almost inevitably have an imbalance of labour which is not matched to your mix and volume. This will result in either service levels dropping because you cannot process the work, or excessive labour bills because staff are under-worked.

When considering standards and productivity in service and administrative environments, it is essential that you are aware of all the work that needs to be done in order to produce your offerings in that setting. In a sense, the first part of standard setting is a definition of the work required. If you imagine a service as a physical product, just like a production line, you are processing information and data into a package which you are selling and/or delivering to your client.

There is no difference between a production shop floor and an insurance company office, in that both are dedicated to the production and delivery of a predefined offering to a customer. There is a predetermined amount of work which needs to be done in both environments to provide a range of offerings and a certain amount of labour-time required to facilitate the delivery of those offerings. If you accept this argument, then it is possible to see that you have the same two standards as in a production environment: "labour" and "output per unit of time".

The process of measuring productivity within a service environment can be broken down into the following steps:

1) Establish a forecast;
2) Define cycle time by process and offering;
3) Define the process required to deliver the offering;
4) Establish process capacity requirement;
5) Define process Takt time to meet cycle time and capacity requirements;

6) Man-load and balance the process, to enable volume, mix and capacity target to be met.

As you can see, there is a substantial and on-going workload in order to measure and manage productivity within a service environment effectively. This requirement for continuous measurement and adjustment is one of the major reasons why so many service-based organisations are inherently unbalanced when it comes to work-load or responding to outside customer initiated contact. When organisations try to respond to work balancing issues and they do not have the six steps above in place, there is a tendency to get individual departments engaging in a range of coping strategies, from hiring more staff to cutting back on process, and this is the reason why customer service starts to suffer.

1) Forecast

The forecast is a fairly obvious requirement, as it is inherently difficult to predict what your work load is going to be without one. Yet, it is one of the things few businesses attempt to do on a regular basis. The majority of businesses will produce a quarterly financial forecast, but this is of no use for process capacity planning. For the purposes of this exercise, a forecast must be done at an individual product level and conducted on a weekly basis. It is only at this level of detail that you will become aware of the capacity constraints that affect your processes. Even at a weekly forecast level, you will encounter daily and hourly peaks in your process and it will be necessary to understand the effects these peaks have on staffing within the process. A good starting point would be a weekly forecast by product type and this should allow you to establish the volume of work that is required to be managed by your core business processes.

2) Cycle Time

The next step is to define the cycle time you require for the process you are designing. For example, if you wish to process your mortgage applications within 1 week of submission, then your cycle time might be defined in terms of 5 working days. This would translate into 40 working hours, in terms of processing capacity. This is a very important figure, which we will enlarge upon in the section on capacity later in this chapter.

The key aspect of cycle time is that it is a key determinant of your service contract with your customer and often a key determining factor in the purchasing decision. Service-based organisations have a tendency to define their product or service provision in terms of fulfilment time, and it is due to this practice that so many organisations choose to compete around this factor. Recent innovations in insurance provision have led to "disruptive technologies" allowing almost immediate provision of insurance, through the use of computer technology and the internet. This is a present-day example of technology leading to a dramatic reduction in cycle time provision with an almost infinite increase in capacity. If you are an insurance provider who has not yet adopted this technological innovation, then it will be highly likely that your current processes and systems will soon be redundant. That is not to say that cycle time is everything; there comes a point where the laws of diminishing returns overcome the benefits of reduced cycle time. Other factors, such as service, quality of provision, customisation and personalisation are all potentially as important. Indeed, there are examples of businesses which have dramatically reduced their cycle time, only to realise that the customer is not time sensitive.

For the purpose of measurement, cycle time is broken down into two elements (as with the production environment): theoretical cycle time and actual cycle time. Companies often struggle to measure actual cycle time because the addition of re-work into the actual cycle time increases the overall cycle time considerably and has a negative effect on the process overall. I take the position that faulty offerings should be sidelined into another "exceptions" process. This separation of good and bad offerings allows two things to happen. Firstly, the true quality of the core process is not undermined by re-work and, secondly, it is possible to analyse the re-work for root-cause issues which can lead to improvements in the core process. If this is done properly, a true quality rate for the core process can be established as well as a true cycle time, or Takt time, for right-first-time work. One final point to mention with regard to this separation of work into two discrete processes is that it allows you to pick up on changes to mix and volume within the process much more quickly, without having the added complexity of re-work. The objective of the business will always be to reduce quality issues to zero and this methodology allows this to happen.

3) Process

This element requires the use of process mapping in order to define the individual steps required to accomplish the service offer in question.

4) Capacity

For a capacity plan to be built for your processes, you will need to establish the total work content within the process. In order to do this you will have to follow the process of setting standard times and crewing for each element of work within the process. What is required here is an Earned Standard Labour Hours figure for each service offering. At this stage in the development of your new process that is all it will do; it will not tell you where the labour needs to be deployed, just that you need X-hundred hours in order to process the forecast as it stands. You will then, in all probability, add (on average) 11% extra standard hours to cover holidays and probably another 8% to cover absenteeism. Finally, you will probably add 20% for productivity losses and unexpected work. You need to add these allowances in at this stage in order to avoid being under-staffed as holidays and sickness are always present and people rarely run at 100% of standard for all sorts of reasons.

Now that you have established the total amount of work required in terms of ESLHs from the forecast, you can match it to your available hours. For example, let's say that product A requires 150 ESLHs to complete; you now know that your target cycle time is 40 hours (5 working days). Therefore, if one person were to process product A, it would take him or her 3.75 weeks or 18.75 days. Clearly, this would not be sufficient to meet the cycle time requirement; therefore, we have to work out how many people could handle the 150 hours of work within a week. In this case, we know it to be 3.75 people, but as we can't hire one quarter of a person we round this up to 4 people. That way we know that 4 people can handle the 150 standard hours of work. You may adjust some of your allowances if you have to round-up in such a manner.

5/6) Takt Time and Manloading

Takt time is a German term (*Taktzeit*) for cycle time and what is colloquially called a "drumbeat". It is integrally tied into the concept of demand smoothing and level scheduling in production environments. In a service environment, you will have established a forecast and cycle time for a range of offerings and established the total work content for the process. However, you will still need to allocate work to people within the process. The easiest way to do this is to work out how long one person would take to deliver the entire offering. If that person can do the whole thing within the 5 days specified, this is a bonus. However, it does mean that you need highly trained people to accomplish this, and they might not be available at the price point at which your product is established. Instead, you may find that the total amount of work requires 8 people to achieve the cycle time of five days. You will therefore need to spread the work out equally amongst the team, assigning different tasks to each person and ensuring that they can accomplish the necessary volume and mix required of them. By doing this, you will have effectively established a Takt time for each person or station in the process.

An easy way of understanding this is as follows: imagine each day as a step in the process of delivery of a product to the customer. It might be, for example, that 1 person can handle all the work coming in on day one, but on day two, when credit checks are required, the amount of work requires 2 people. On day three, 2 people are needed in order to conduct searches and type up the applications, and on days four and five only 1 person is required. You have effectively balanced the work out over the 5 days and assigned the correct amount of labour to each step, in order to handle the respective work loads on each of these days/steps in the process. By working through the process in this way and assigning labour to different tasks according to their ESLH requirements, you have smoothed the process and, by manipulating the labour content at each stage, maintained the Takt time through the process, thus avoiding any bottlenecks.

If you cannot make the work fit into buckets of a day and find you have, perhaps, a 6 day process instead, you may need to re-engineer the process in order that it fits the desired Takt time. This may involve re-designing the product is some way, or finding a way of incorporating some of the work within other steps in the process; this may increase staffing.

You should be able to see by now, that this is a moveable feast and is subject to almost continuous change. However, what should be remembered is that in low margin/high volume processes, not manipulating the process to fit the workload and simply "throwing labour" at the problem will quickly lead to insolvency.

In the list above, I separated the process into six steps in order to clarify the process but, as you can see, many of the decisions from step 4 onwards are less discrete and are, in fact, iterative. As a result, you tend to end up doing steps 4-6 all at once and more or less continually.

The Productivity Calculation

This may seem a very long-winded approach, to what is effectively the same calculation as in a production environment, but I think it's important that you know how you construct the process, as it lends credence to the measure itself.

Example:

As in the calculation for production, we start with the number of standard labour hours required for each product being handled by the process. Let's say, for argument's sake, that in this case all products use 8 people, for 5 days, at 8 hours a day, producing 250 products or applications. The standards would, therefore, be 250 products per 40 hours, or 6.25 products an hour, with a standard crew of 8 people.

The first step is to calculate the *standard time*. This is the time it should take for an offering to be processed from beginning to end. It is calculated using the following formula:

$$\sum \left[\frac{\textit{Units produced}}{\textit{Standard units per unit of production time}} \right]$$

In our example, we processed 150 product offerings in the first week. We know that we should be able to process 6.25 product offerings per hour, therefore if we divide 150 units by our standard rate of 6.25, we see that it should have taken 24 hours of work to complete these offerings.

$$\sum \frac{150}{6.25} = 24 \textit{ hrs}$$

Now that we have out standard time, it is possible to work out how much standard labour we should have used. We know that the standard crew for the process is 8 people; therefore, we can multiply the 8 people by 24 hours or standard work to arrive at an "Earned Standard Labour Hours" (ESLH) figure. In this case, 24*8 = 192 hours.

The figure of 192 hours, is how many hours of labour you should have paid for, in order to produce the 150 offerings that week. Unfortunately, all 8 people were employed for the full week of 39 hours each, which means you paid for 39*8 = 312 labour hours.

Now that you have these crucial two bits of information (ESLHs and Actual Labour Hours) you are in a position to calculate your productivity using the following formula:

$$Productivity = \sum \left[\frac{ESLH}{Actual\ Hours} \right]$$

$$\sum \frac{192}{312} = 61.5\%$$

As you can see, this translates into a productivity figure of 61.5% This effectively means you have paid almost 40% more than you should have done to provide the product offering through the process - a significant opportunity for improvement.

Chapter 7

DOWNTIME IN PRODUCTION ENVIRONMENTS

"Waste is worse than loss. The time is coming when every person who lays claim to ability will keep the question of waste before him constantly."

Thomas Edison

If you are measuring productivity in your business, then you are, by default, also measuring efficiency.

$$Efficiency = \sum \left[\frac{Standard\ time}{Actual\ time\ used} \right]$$

Productivity is influenced by two things: efficiency and the amount of labour used. Unless you are using the incorrect amount of labour on a line, you will undoubtedly be looking to efficiency as the major cause of loss in performance and "downtime" is the major factor in this. Downtime is time which should have been used to produce something but, for one reason or another, has not. Generally, I find that in most organisations there is a general hierarchy to the priority paid to productivity and efficiency related issues. This hierarchy has evolved over many years of practice, and is summarised in the following diagram.

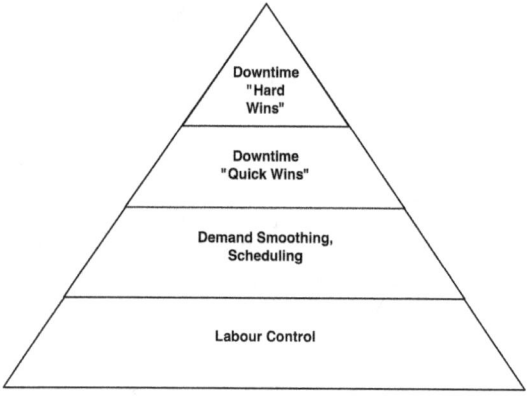

There will be purists who will disagree with this view, but the only argument I can see against using this bottom-up approach is the amount of time you would spend on each step.□4 For example, if you work in an organisation with little labour, then many of the productivity benefits of labour control and standardisation will not be available to you; however, it should still be the starting point. Demand smoothing and scheduling further enhance productivity and eliminate the largest chunk of efficiency related downtime. Once these first two steps have been achieved, you will have done everything you can for production in terms of providing them with a stable and predictable demand pattern with the correct amount of labour and control to deliver it. It is at this stage that downtime becomes a priority. Any focus on downtime before these first two steps have been achieved will be difficult to sustain. It is one of the reasons that a major emphasis in this book is on standards, as without them there is no foundation upon which to build operational improvement activities.

Broadly speaking, downtime is split into the

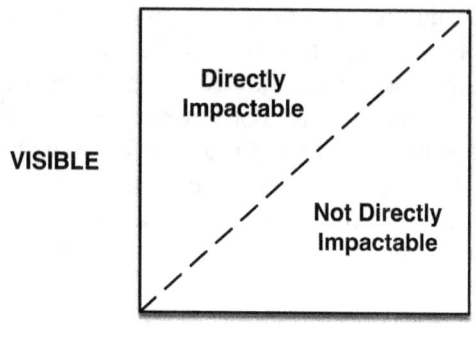

INVISIBLE

following categories:

We are used to thinking of downtime in terms of things we can easily identify and see, such as the machinery stopping or raw materials not being available for processing. However, there is also another category of downtime which is not visible, for instance planning and scheduling rules. All downtime categories are more or less impactable to varying degrees depending on where you work within an operation. For the operator on a production line, the supply chain rules are both invisible and not directly impactable; however, to the planning department they may be visible and impactable.

The premise of any measurement system is to inform the present and, if possible, the near future, so that action can be taken to ensure that what happens next is predictable and, if possible, better than the past.

If you accept this definition of a measurement system, then you will agree that in order to ensure things improve going forward, action must be taken as soon as possible. Therefore, we measure in order to inform action. I cannot emphasise this enough; I have come across so many organisations which measure everything but fail to **DO** anything. Measurement is impotent without the capability to implement.

Lost Time

"Lost Time" is another expression you will come across when dealing with downtime. Lost time is actually a balancing figure, which represents the downtime that you may not be able to account for.

Calculation:

Lost Time (mins) = [Production Time – Standard Time – Downtime]

As an example, we have a process which ran for 120 minutes. The standard time for the process was 60 minutes (50% efficiency) and during this time it stopped for 45 minutes. For some unexplainable reason the team leader on the line only noticed 15 minutes of that downtime and, as a result, only recorded 15 minutes downtime on his control sheet. The calculation would therefore be:

Lost time = [120 minutes - 60 minutes - 15 minutes] = 45 minutes

This would mean that lost time would equal 45 minutes; in other words, 45 minutes of production time are unaccounted for.

You can see that if you did not do this calculation and relied only on the observations of the team leader, you would be under the impression that the line had only lost 15 minutes of production. Using this calculation allows us to see the hidden, or unobserved, downtime on a line and is, therefore, very valuable to the management team when looking at production losses.

There are many reason why this may have occurred, but in my experience it is mainly "rate loss": either through the loss of good product due to scrap, or as a result of the machine running at less than the full standard rate.

Once again, standards and standard time are fundamental in the accurate control and accounting of the process.

It's important to understand that lost time is the balancing figure which keeps the productivity calculation honest. It's almost a number which shouts, "Hey, I know we have productivity and downtime, but we are still not accounting for a load of stuff!" In that sense, this is a powerful measure of system compliance and accuracy, and should be regarded as such.

Paretos

There is a long history of turning downtime into Pareto diagrams, but it is not the intention of this book to go into detail of how these are constructed. The reason for mentioning them here is that it is very easy to measure downtime in minutes and then focus on the largest causes of downtime in this way. I have seen enough examples where this has been misleading. Downtime should be measured as a percentage of run time for the line or machine it refers to. In addition, in some production environments certain lines produce incredibly high value components, whilst other do not. Therefore, it is worth considering attaching some form of value to the line where the downtime occurs.

I have seen examples where relatively small amounts of downtime - which would not have been the focus of any remedial action because the team would have focused on the bigger items higher up the Pareto - suddenly become big ticket items.

Chapter 8

DOWNTIME IN NON-PRODUCTION ENVIRONMENTS

Downtime in a service environment follows the same principles as in a production environment, but with one major difference. Most of the downtime in a service environment is, to a greater degree, invisible. There will, of course, always be the elements of downtime that are easily identifiable, such as meetings, coffee breaks, comfort breaks, personal calls, extended lunch breaks, sickness, absenteeism, and so forth. The main challenge in a service environment is rate loss, and this is simply due to the nature of the process.

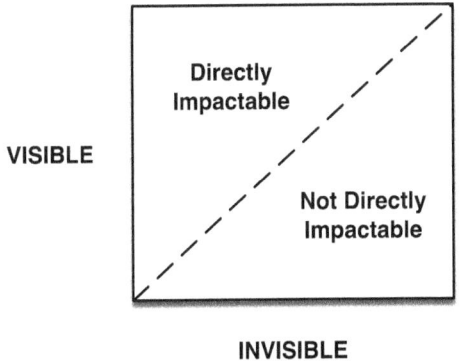

A simple example of what I mean can be illustrated through careful analysis of anyone who has to interact with a computer as part of his or her work process. During an average day, computer systems will fluctuate in speed depending on the bandwidth/latency available and the amount of users. The speed difference might be as little as one or two percent (or, as I have seen, up to fifty percent or more). One or two percent may not seem a critical amount to worry about, but if you are processing a million applications a year that would translate into 20,000 pieces of business you didn't process in that year, the equivalent of giving all your staff a week off. Simply because the net annualised effect only relates to a few minutes a day does not mean that the overall effect on your annual profitability is not a substantial one and not worthy of further study.

One of the other major factors in service-based industries is the volatility of demand. Human behaviour being what it is, if you do not have enough work for people, they will find things to fill their time, such as extra coffee breaks and slowing the pace of work. This behaviour is natural. The problem arises when people are asked to speed up to the required Takt time again. Staff are unable to judge the required pace of the ramp-up and consequently under-estimate the requirements; as a result, they incur downtime in the form of rate loss. If, like some businesses, you reach peak capacity in your process at month end or at the end of a sales cycle, you will constantly subject your staff to variable work rates. As a result of this type of commercial behaviour, you will constantly have to balance capacity (in the form of man-hours) against quality (in the form of on-time-in-full delivery). One of the ways of avoiding this is to ensure a stable and predictable supply of work, or to flex the working hours to suit the demand fluctuations.

I suggested in chapter 6 that you take re-work off-line in a service environment. The reason for this is that it is very difficult to establish the cause of issues within the core process when the core process itself is having to cope with re-work. Causal reasons tend to be better analysed separately and then investigated within the core process. This way you do not waste any of your valuable capacity in the core process and you maintain the ability to isolate issues as they arise. If you leave re-work and faulty work within the core process, operators will try to re-work issues occurring in the process and reduce the capacity and takt time of the core process. In these circumstances, it has been known for people to resort to process mapping the entire process to find out what operators are doing that they shouldn't be doing. If an operator is left to re-work issues within a process, then over time this re-work will be viewed as an integral part of the core process. If this is then taught to new operators, it very quickly becomes the *de facto* standard for the process. If this happens, you lose the ability for operators to report issues accurately. The first signs of this occurring are usually found in staff turnover figures. Employees will leave if they can see that they are working ineffectively and are under pressure, especially if they feel that they cannot rectify this situation.

As a result, if you take exceptions out of the process, you should only be left with genuine downtime issues such as system downtime and loss of available hours to extra-ordinary activities such as training and meetings.

Example of rate loss

I have mentioned rate loss as a major issue in service environments in this chapter. What follows is an example of rate loss and how you can include the extra labour associated with coping with it in the overall productivity calculation. The reason for showing this is that I have recommended taking work out of the core process. This is quite a different approach to that taken in production environments, where this is rarely possible.

Rate loss also includes re-work. If, out of 150 product offerings mentioned in the example in chapter 6, 50 are classed as re-work going through the re-work process and there are 5 people employed in the re-work area, you would need to amend the overall productivity calculation to reflect this. The easiest way to do this is to add the 5 extra people to your actual paid hours and reflect the number of good applications cleared through the re-work process.

In this example, out of 150 cleared applications last week, 50 were returned due to quality issues, and out of the 50 returned, 35 were cleared and fixed and re-worked. What is the overall productivity of the group?

Your standard hours would be as follows: you produced 100 good products (instead of the 150 in the previous example) and, had you done so at the standard rate of 6.25 an hour, you would have consumed $100/6.25 = 16$ hours of time. You then multiply your standard time by your standard crew to see how many labour hours you should have used. This is then $16*8 = 128$ standard labour hours. At the end of the week you find out you paid for 8 crew for 40 hours, or 320 man-hours. This means your core process was $128/320 = 40\%$ productive. To calculate the group's total productivity you do the following:

Since the re-work team managed to re-work 35 of the 50 bad applications, you achieved 135 good products/applications in the week. Therefore, your standard hours were $135/6.25 = 21.6$ hours. You should have used 8 people, so ESLHs were $21.6*8 = 172.8$. Instead, you used 13 people for 40 hours, or 520 man-hours, so your total productivity was $172.8/520 = 33.2\%$.

Chapter 9

3-2-1 REPORTING

You really can't write a book about KPIs and not talk about 3-2-1 reporting. This is an idea as old as the hills and is probably a cast back to more bureaucratic times. However, the principles at play here are as relevant today as ever they were, indeed probably more so.

The basic premise goes along the lines as follows: the higher up an organisation you are, the greater the spread of your responsibility with regard to the number of operations under your control. If you were to try to manage all of your operations at the same level as a supervisor on the shop floor, you would be overwhelmed with information and, as a result, rapidly become ineffective, as you would not be able to see the wood from the trees. Rather than trying to look at all the KPIs from all of your operations individually, you would benefit from just looking at one aggregated KPI for the totality of your operations. If that KPI does not meet your expectations, you can then identify which operation(s) has caused the issue and invite the manager from that operation in for a meeting to explain what has gone wrong. This then allows you to manage by exception. If this works properly, people do not get micro-managed by their superiors and poor performers receive the support and challenge required to deliver better results.

This sounds great and when it works it does work brilliantly. However, with the constant restructuring of organisations and the incessant changing of roles and responsibilities, it is hard to do in practice. If you add on personalities and ambition, it is not hard to see how, within a relatively short period of time, a perfect 3-2-1 reporting system can end up disjointed and failing.

3-2-1 reporting gets more difficult in matrix organisations because the natural hierarchy of the KPIs is not so apparent. With the advent of modern IT systems, most employees and managers today have access to more information than ever before. If you take just these two aspects of modern business, it is no surprise to see people wallowing in unstructured data. In a way, the progress we have made in business agility has been undone by our lack of rigidity with regard to our reporting structure. In fact, whether or not the organisation is a matrix, the same level of discipline that a hierarchical structure required in the past is still needed. This may seem contradictory in the context of agility; however, as with standards (see chapter 2), it is the fixed nature of the standards that allows us to see how agile we are. I like to think that modern business is a bit like trying to measure the speed of a river, whilst you are floating down the middle of it: you catch glimpses of trees on the bank as you speed by, but are unable to measure speed, distance and direction due to the lack of fixed reference points.

In the coming decade, we shall find that the fluidity of our business models and the speed of change will make our need for fixed reference points all the more necessary. The challenge for us is to find ways of allowing the changes to occur, whilst maintaining clarity over the direction, speed and scale of change.

In summary, an important element of the construction of a productivity measure is the structure of the data within the organisation. It is not enough simply to have a productivity measure; you also need to ensure that the correct people are reviewing it, at the correct time interval, and at the right level of aggregation. One of the foundation blocks which ensures the success of 3-2-1 reporting within an organisation is application of "Roles, Responsibilities and

Accountabilities." These will be covered briefly in the next chapter.

Chapter 10

ROLES, RESPONSIBILITIES AND ACCOUTABILITIES

"A person may cause evil to others not only by his actions but by his inaction, and in either case he is justly accountable to them for injury."

John Stuart Mill

It is always a surprise to me, how few people are aware of their responsibilities in a business environment. They are normally able to tell me what their job title is and describe the main body of their work. Few, if any, when asked if they have a job description and whether it is up-to-date are able to produce this document or hold it in any sort of credence. Surprisingly, I find that perhaps one of the largest contributors to work stress is the lack of definition around roles and responsibilities. I have seen dozens of employees in tears of gratitude once I have established an up-to-date job description with clear roles, responsibilities and accountabilities.

Not surprisingly, there seems little point in undertaking a huge exercise within a business to create a KPI such as productivity, if, on conclusion, you have an entire organisation unsure of who should be responsible for the measurement. All measurement systems require maintenance in order to function correctly. Data, by its very nature, degrades as it is rarely totally independent and, as a result, left to its own devices will start to corrupt. I have found that the only real way of maintaining data is to ensure that people are dependent on the output from the data to perform their role effectively. This way, if the data starts to lose its accuracy, people will notice and make efforts to maintain its integrity. However, if no one is responsible or accountable for a data set, this is unlikely to happen; it often becomes a case of "I thought someone else was doing that".

For years, businesses have used, what is commonly termed, a RACI matrix in order to establish a structured approach to define the roles and responsibilities in relation to organisational KPIs. RACI stands for "Responsible", "Accountable", "Consulted" and "Informed". As a form of classification it works well and affords a level of clarity to all employees concerned. Along with this acronym are some basic definitions to help you decide what your relationship should be with a certain KPI, and these are as follows:

Responsible - These are people who have the ability to change a KPI's performance. If you drive a car, you are responsible for the speed at which you drive, as it is your foot on the accelerator. Sometimes senior managers feel responsible for performance but, unless they are actually doing the job of their employees, they are not responsible; they will instead be accountable.

Accountable - Most managers are accountable for the performance of a KPI. Although they cannot directly drive the car, they are accountable for what the car ultimately does. As a result, in most managerial cases, they will manage the people responsible for a KPI, whilst maintaining accountability for the actions of their employees and the performance of the process.

Informed - These are people who receive KPI information for which they have no responsibility or accountability, but have an interest in the KPI itself. For example, finance is rarely responsible or accountable for site productivity, but because site productivity will affect the profitability of the business, they are often informed of the KPI.

I have deliberately left out "consulted" as I believe it is misleading. I think that if you have to consult someone in relation to a KPI, then you are in some way creating a level of accountability in that person because of the advice he/she is giving you. This muddies the waters and I cannot see any reason for formalising a process of advice gathering within the business. Informal networks and advice giving is not a formal process in most organisations. In the twenty odd years I have been working with organisations, I have, in almost all cases, managed to get only RAI into businesses with any level of success. In the future, as organisations become increasingly flatter, there is a good argument for bringing responsibility and accountability together, under one banner.

It is important to note that RACI does work well in project tasking. On the internet, there are discussions which praise the usefulness of RACI where it is applied to tasking. In this chapter, however, I am applying it to KPIs, not project tasking.

Chapter 11

PLANNING FOR PRODUCTIVITY

> *"Planning is required when the future state that we desire involves a set of interdependent decisions; that is, a system of decisions . . . the principle complexity in planning derives from the interrelatedness of the decisions rather than from the decisions themselves . . ."*

Russell Ackoff, 1970

One of the largest benefits of the productivity measure in manufacturing is the ability to forecast, with surprising accuracy, the amount and cost of labour required to deliver a forecast. The importance of this will differ depending on the amount of labour used in the manufacturing process. Some industries, such as micro-electronics, consume labour in such a small percentage in relation to their total manufacturing costs that productivity plays a much smaller role as a measure. However, in the case of many FMCG businesses, where thousands are employed on the shop floor on a daily basis and can account for more than 30% of the total site costs, this measure is very important. As we have seen in the section on non-production environments, productivity is a fundamental measure no matter what the headcount, as the dependency on high cost labour to enable service levels is key to the success and profitability of the business.

Now those of you who are planners, or have much to do with planning, will immediately question my motivation in this chapter. After all, we all know that net machine efficiency is the metric we use for planning, don't we?

Well, technically you are correct, but it is only half the equation. Net machine efficiency will give you capacity and run time, but it will not give you the amount of labour resource required to accomplish the task; that ultimately falls to productivity. Remember that productivity is the division of Earned Standard Labour Hours by actual hours consumed; efficiency only works with standard machine hours and actual machine hours, and does not deal with the labour element at all. Therefore, if you are putting a budget together for the next financial year and you want next year's labour requirement to be accurate, you should run your forecast against your standards database to work out the total number of standard labour hours required. You should then divide that number by you average productivity, and the resulting figure will give you the total number of actual hours required to accomplish that production at a given rate of productivity. Because productivity uses total hours paid for, the number includes set-up times, change-overs, clean-downs, breaks, and all the other associated time that goes with bringing in a crew to run a line.

Quite simply, you cannot make net machine efficiency do the same job, even if you tried to take total efficiency as your number. I have seen people try to take a percentage of production value to try to estimate labour; others have relied on forms of voodoo involving fag packets and chicken bones. In the twenty years I have been doing this, I have found only one way to do this correctly and this is with productivity. Unfortunately, it requires a great deal of systemic development to allow you, as the planner and forecaster, to access the necessary numbers. However, there is a silver lining if you are reading this as a senior manager, as it means that you have three extra ways of applying the necessary pressure in your organisation to develop good management systems: planning, finance and human resources. All of these departments have a vested interest in having the productivity measurement within the business.

The planning department needs it to estimate the daily and "shiftly" labour requirements, so that only the correct amount of labour comes in on shift for the correct amount of time. Human resources need it to know what the future requirements of the business are in order to hire more (or fewer) people and to arrange appropriate training. Finance, as we have already mentioned, needs it to know so that it can budget accurately and estimate the future profitability of the business. So you see, in some ways, productivity, rather than being just a shop floor measure, is one of the core measures of the business, depended on by just about everyone. Yet in my experience, due to the complexity of implementing the measure, it remains largely abandoned by the majority of businesses.

In our experience, we have seen some remarkable financial performance improvements as a result of making the effort to use productivity in planning. On a global supply chain basis, savings/improvements can be measured in the 10s of millions, and in individual manufacturing sites we have seen 2-3% EBIT improvements.

One of the surprising things about forecasting your labour requirement in this way is just how stable productivity seems to be in most organisations. There seems to be a rate of productivity with which an organisation is happy to work. As a result, I have found over the years that the financial forecast tends to be quite robust and achievable. This will be music to the ears of anyone, who is responsible for the delivery of budgets. One of the other advantages of using this measurement is that people cannot use mix or volume as an excuse for not hitting target, as you are tying labour to work in the workplace as a ratio. Therefore, as long as productivity targets are met, you are assured of the correct ratio of labour usage, in spite of fluctuations in demand and mix. Unfortunately, too many organisations seem to regard labour as a fixed cost and, therefore, each budget review is a cause for much wailing and gnashing of teeth over labour variances.

Another use of productivity in planning is in the variances that it produces. For example, if your best administrator can cope with a certain quantity of work, and it is his/her output that you use as the standard to judge all other administrators doing the same work, you will quickly be able to identify the capability of the other staff against your benchmark. This sort of information can be used effectively to plan extra training in order to improve performance. Alternatively, it allows you to price the cost of a transaction accurately, which enables you to look carefully at, for example, outsourcing proposals. One of the reasons why so many outsourcing contracts fail to deliver the expected results is due to imprecise measurement of standard work and the lack of measurement of the "exceptionals" that occur. It is often the case that if the outsourced contract only handled right-first-time business, the savings quoted at the outset would be realised. Unfortunately, the 25%+ exceptions to the core process is where all of the cost is incurred. Ideally, accurate measurement would allow you to identify the cost of exceptions and engineer an in-house solution. This would either remove the need to outsource or, at the very least, mean that outsourcing would deliver on its promise.

In production environments I have found that if you remove all constraints from the planning process and create a "perfect schedule", most companies that work seven days a week, 24 hours a day will be able to achieve their total production targets in three days. It is the focus on productivity and its associated cost savings which allows people to consider this type of scenario. All of the shift premiums, overtime, triple time and four days of labour all but disappear in this scenario. All that is left is the necessary actions required of the supply chain in order to facilitate such a change.

End Notes

[1] This is a very useful bit of information, which many companies do not have in their day-to-day operations. Many companies simply work on an average of their weekly labour bill divided by the number of production days in the week. In our research, we have seen a daily variation of labour requirements in excess of 20% on average, not including weekend work where partial production is undertaken. Most of this variation can be attributed to volume and mix changes within the week, brought about either by customer forecast or by internal scheduling rules. In a £20m FMCG business with a labour bill of 20%, this normally equates to an average improvement on the labour bill of £600,000 before efficiency improvements. I mention this only to draw your attention to how big the savings can be, once you take control of your standards and measurement processes in your business. Clearly, the larger your business, the larger the potential savings.

[2] It is important to remember that this is profit that you have lost, which cannot be regained. At the end of each year, this number is often measured in the millions of pounds, and is often the difference between a business that is able to re-invest in itself and pay staff bonuses, and one that faces cutbacks in the following financial year.

[3] In this chapter, I refer to the output within a service environment as an 'offering' simply because it is easier to refer to some generic output in this manner, and it will make reading easier.

[4] Modern, service-based industries which rely heavily on people to deliver their offerings will find that labour control and demand smoothing make up a disproportionate amount of time, with regard to downtime reduction.

About Finidhyn

We are living through possibly the biggest revolution in work and business practice since the industrial revolution. In the next twenty years, we will move to a dis-aggregated, de-averaged, dis-intermediated, deconstructed world that is networked and seamless. Time will no longer interrupt business process globally and the risks associated with this global 24-hour business environment will continue to magnify.

Modern business is complex, fast moving and unforgiving. Business has grown beyond the individual's ability to master it; modern management is about integrated systemic management techniques. Modern businesses are complex adaptive systems within which old deterministic and Newtonian mind-sets will fail to deliver the solutions required in the future.

Finidhyn is a creative, innovative, boutique operational business improvement and software company. It has become synonymous with the delivery of solutions in "unbounded" or complex business scenarios. Finidhyn pioneered an end-to-end design and delivery process for corporate transformation that is regarded as the benchmark tool for transformative change in global corporations. Finidhyn offer an alternative to the cookie-cutter approach of traditional business advice and, as a result, demonstrate results far beyond the reach of the rest of the market.

Specialisations

- Change Management
- Operational Strategy
- Supply Chain Optimisation
- Planning
- Value Chain Deconstruction
- Lean Manufacturing
- Building Management Systems
- Project Implementation
- Process Engineering
- Business Process Improvement
- Business Valuation
- Productivity Improvement
- Business Turnaround
- Operational Due Diligence
- SEO Data Analytics and Design
- Software Design and Delivery
- Contract Review
- Operational Analysis
- Business Feasibility Studies
- Market Feasibility Studies

NOTES